SPARROW

SADE RUSDEN

SPARROW

A POETRY
COLLECTION

Drifted Feather Press

To my little bird,
My Sparrow who travels through the forest—
and meadows of my heart.
Who will continue over the waters and through
the galaxy of my soul.

healing

*your personal summit calls for you to
echo upon its peaks*

essential

i don't just crave for my body to be immersed in water
i need it
like one needs their daily vitamins
this is my serving
this is my dose
my body will always speak to me
it is time
it has been too long
you need a body of water to plunge into
instantly I am replenished
mind, body and spirit
reaping the benefits of the moment
i make way to the surface
i am no longer lacking anything essential

vital

i don't ever want to be detached
from any body of water
i want to become one with it
as if it were my own body
showing me how to move
how to feel
how to pour myself out
how to give
how to be lighter than the weight of the world
i float peering up at the sky
being one with the wavelet
i can finally see
i would glide over every stone just to soak it all up
every drop
every last drop

moonlit footsteps

it's during the nightly moon
where my footsteps are in secret
upon stone
upon the earth
embraced by the presence of
alpine tree silhouettes
where the roof above my head is the stars
every move i make i search for the moon
between the height of the branches
a longing that is always fulfilled
once sighted i am fully aligned

holy water

embracing the droplets
cascading from the heavens
trying to reach my mind
making its way through
the span of branches and pine needles
until reaching my skin
sliding down the slopes of my body
freshening my soul
i am not meant to run for absolute cover
i am asked to soak up its blessing
when it's time
i am recharged from heaven's touch
i am showered with holy water

goodbye —
the wings to the bones
that have been aching

forget me not

where did you leave yourself
in the dust of your current thoughts
in daily tasks that cost being lost
don't forget about yourself
have you forgotten your love for a hike
for time in solitude
for your words to be written down
for your passions
don't forget about yourself
when you cease to pursue all
that excites your heart
all that soothes your heart
you neglect yourself
you reject your authentic self

sentimental town

she hasn't felt this way since she left her beloved
neighborhood behind
with her new path that sets upon
the foothills of hope
she feels it run through her
walking amongst the evergreens and cherry trees
walking like she used to every day
in the depth of the tropical valley
passing friendly faces
tending to their homes and gardens
a sense of familiarity arises
and she feels that her soul smiles
the soft pastel sunset leads her way
the view of the vast lake
ledges of lingering mountains
she is reminded of her ocean
perhaps this is her home away from home
at least for now
no matter where she ends up
she has a sneaking suspicion that she will revisit
this new home time and time again
for how can she dishonor what it has given her
by treating it like it never existed
like it never healed her

prey

the claws are in you
the fangs are imbedded in you
remove the weapon and venom
but live with the punctures
for at least those will heal

cliffs

I hid on the cliffs
hoping to not take that unforgiving plummet
yet I'd rather have clung to dear life
than to have offered it up to the one
that would torture my soul

desolate

the spirits cascade
into the crevasses of the desert clay
wind picking up the sand
making it feel like needles being aimed at my face
all i want is for my thirst to be quenched
my tongue licks the salt off my lips
i am longing
i am searching on my knees
blindly feeling with arms stretched out
hoping to feel for something worth holding onto
and then i see it
the glare of water shimmering from the extreme heat
my spirit picks my heavy bones up
and i run to the glimpse of hope
i fall into the water
i pledge my thanks
my thirst is quenched
my body and mind may have seemed broken at times
yet my spirit made me survive
the love of a desolate desert

rose garden

when it's my time to sleep for good
i want to be buried below my rose garden
i want to be incorporated into the roots
so that when you care to pick an imperfectly
perfect rose you will be holding me too
and as each petal shall fall
in the warmth of your home
among my grandchildren
you will return to pick another
and i'll be happy you came back to visit
so that i can be a part of your life
long after i am gone

growth

*a spirit with stamina is one that will outlast
any of life's marathons*

hummingbird

flying backwards
only for a second
for these wings move
too fast to stay
wings of speed that make my beat
humming a special tune to keep
attracted to red they say but i love the blue that i am
i need sweetness to survive
nectar needing to be collected
replenish
balance
seek
this is my repeat

burst

crave to be beneath the sky that changes
the sky that welcomes your gaze
with an endless array of colors
colors mixed from heaven's hand
where a shade of pink can be as delicate
as the blushing mini rose
it can be a blazing fiery red that mocks a fire
it can be a smokey grey that isn't lonely
when it's paired with the warmth of amber
it can be a vibrant purple with hues of blue
that blend into a display of cotton candy
an everyday occurrence that brings you to your knees
that helps you to reflect
that fills your heart with gratitude
that elevates your mood
that moves your soul
that gives you the comfort you need
the sunset is not just the night falling upon me
it's the sky pouring into me

stone

abrasion
a necessary process to smooth out each stone
to break existing jagged edges
it is necessary
the rushing waters
the coarse sand
the strong wind
all persist and take part in putting forth the effort
that results in weathering
a stone perfectly smooth does not exist without effort
what would we walk upon as a result?

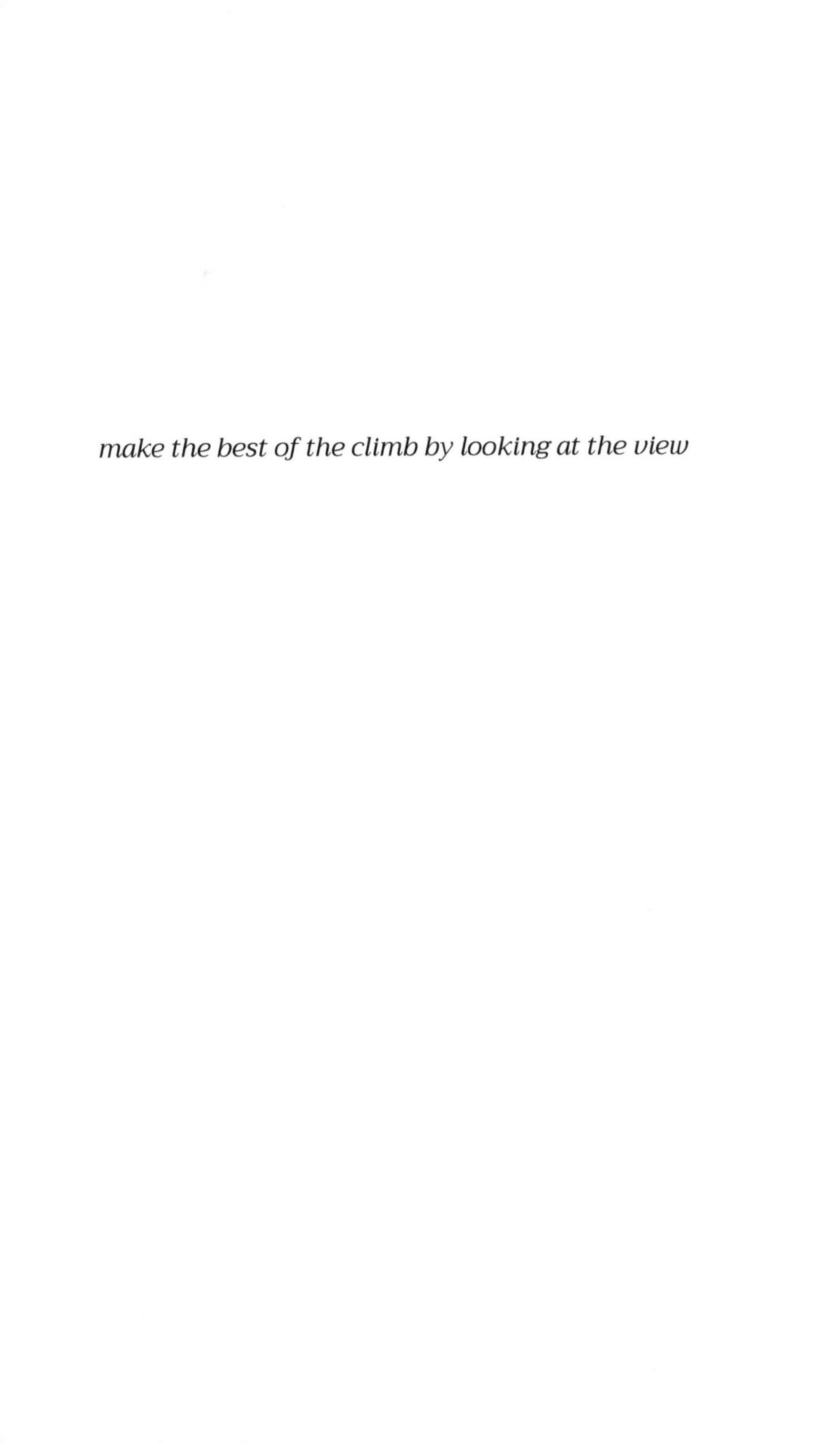
make the best of the climb by looking at the view

silent witness

if trees could share
the amount of secret tales they witnessed
the kiss between those two young lovebirds
the goodbye that shattered a heart
the building of a family legacy
the playful animals that only had a small
time slot in this life
the fights that were forgiven
the injuries that were tended to
the resting hearts that gave thanks
the wishes whispered of endless aspirations
the prayers made under the shade
the people who were once called friends who never
returned to the bond of a family
if trees could share the stories they peered down upon
we would have a harder time cutting them down

instinct will always
complete a maze

bone graveyard

a maze of deer bones
laced through newly grown trees
leaving its trace
with a predator lurking nearby
i press forward thinking about the
circle of life
how easy it is to turn to
a trail of bones
and yet where those bones lay
new
life
grows

spark

all you need is a glimmer
without the need for a show
of fire and bright lights
just a subtle shining light wavering
can redefine the darkness

voyager

the voyage changes once the long journey
is discovered in a deeper way
a way that seeks the undertow
the mystery of the depths
rather than the surface in which
is so easy for our eyes to see
it is when the voyager dives into the current
that makes it a journey worth discovering

chameleon

it is only natural
to have emotions arise when the world
as you know it
changes
yet you adjust to the shift and the tilt
you adapt just like you were meant to
it is only natural

daisy

find inspiration in the smallest of things
that we often walk over
it's comforting knowing that the soul takes notice
to even the smallest of flowers
we were just about to trample on

rainbow

cascading down like a waterfall from the heavens
there is a message
that must be received
from the angels trying to be clear
through the rainy skies
they depart the clouds
for their signal to be noticed in the heart
of the one who truly catches the rainbow

pass the torch

the wind of the long white cloud
churning its sound
ancestors speak through
carrying me out
with a torch of fire
you are next in line
they say
how are you to live
how are you to leave your legacy
make it known enough
so that the carvings in the stone
can make your name unforgotten
worthy enough to announce
are you leaving your mark
among the voyagers
among the warriors

the fall

floating
citrine-colored leaves
the trees confetti
celebrating
change and renewal
the trees detach from their leaves
letting go
enduring the bareness
only to come back in full
it just took time
to recover from the fall

freedom

forever gravitating toward the mountains
never failing are my feet that take me there

island

gliding over
free
unattached to all that
disconnects me
from this moment
the moment that allows me to see these sights
that can't be bargained with
the water that welcomes me in from a single touch
it's irresistible
from wild roses exploring their island
dainty and sweet
the aroma lures me in
from the birds that reside here
their chimes seem to be the only ones
who know i am here
the sun is setting
i must be getting back
only to soon return to the freeing feeling i get

migration

what may weigh you down today
will be the very thing
that will one day set you free
patience
it's this time that is preparing you
for that moment you can fly again
and when you think you are stuck in this moment
you are really just preparing
yourself for the big migration

pirate

tension is just a passerby
when you have an ocean to explore
and a world to be a pioneer in
you stress not
you claim the sea
you claim what you seek

smoke signals

her river is wild
smoke signals rise
so cling onto your raft
you are about to experience her wrath

escape

unleashed from city limits
i am free in the open land
of the countryside
pure and wild
my heart fastens itself
closely and securely to this
i have no continuous desire to head back
i am too busy listening to the wolves
too busy watching sunsets among the conifers
too busy swimming in pristine water
too busy below the array of stars
too busy harvesting
too busy being in my element
too busy learning from nature
too busy without chains

wild horse

she was free
untouchable in the roaming rolling hills
the terrain was her salvation
with the wind as wild as her spirit
change became
they tried to break her in
boundaries narrowed in around her
every time the reigns are taken to her
she waits for her great escape
her spirit just won't be broken in
for freedom is right on the other side

fire

the smoke from the cedars enwraps and twirl
into the grey sky
a dancing ceremony
the hypnotic fire shines in our eyes
embers whistling
how can something so untouchable
touch our hearts
and our minds
perhaps it is the unstoppable desire
a fire has once it begins burning
once its rhythm is set
mirroring our own inner flames

love

*the sun and the water a
magnetic romance*

mother to daughter

i want to share this life
in these moments of adventure
with you
i want your eyes to marvel in the beauty of this world
i want you to always crave to get out
so that you never feel stuck
life has too much to offer
and i want to serve it to you on a platter
so that your heart is full
not just by beauty
but by the memories you create
with your mother
and the lessons that come with it
i want you to know
what may seem ordinary
usually ends up being what is truly extraordinary
now let's continue
to share this flight

lioness

fierce in the way i touch in the way i climb
in how i crawl my way out
fierce in my way of keeping moments
that can't be lost
fierce in the way i give my heart
in the way i protect
fierce in what i search for in passion
that needs to expand in optimism
that can be a rarity
yet tender from the all of it from all that ignites
my fire from all that i honor

nothing without

what is a sunset
without the passion for it
what is a meadow
without the curiosity of the flowers
what is a lake
without the willingness to discover
what is a breeze
without the enjoyment of it
what is a sacred valley
without the respect for it

hunter

call me by a distant echo
track me down with hunger
follow my scent
until it pairs with yours
dusk to dawn
hunt me

a rose and her thorns

belle with a presence
delicate yet with a weapon
soft yet hardy
passionate with the ability to puncture
if one wants her to flourish
with the beauty they fell in love with
in the first place
you must accept her thorns

no holding back

intimidation is often times just a facade
once you gain familiarity the sense of fear
subsides and the tide rises
to release and relieve you from the drawback
to fully enjoy the flow you were missing out on

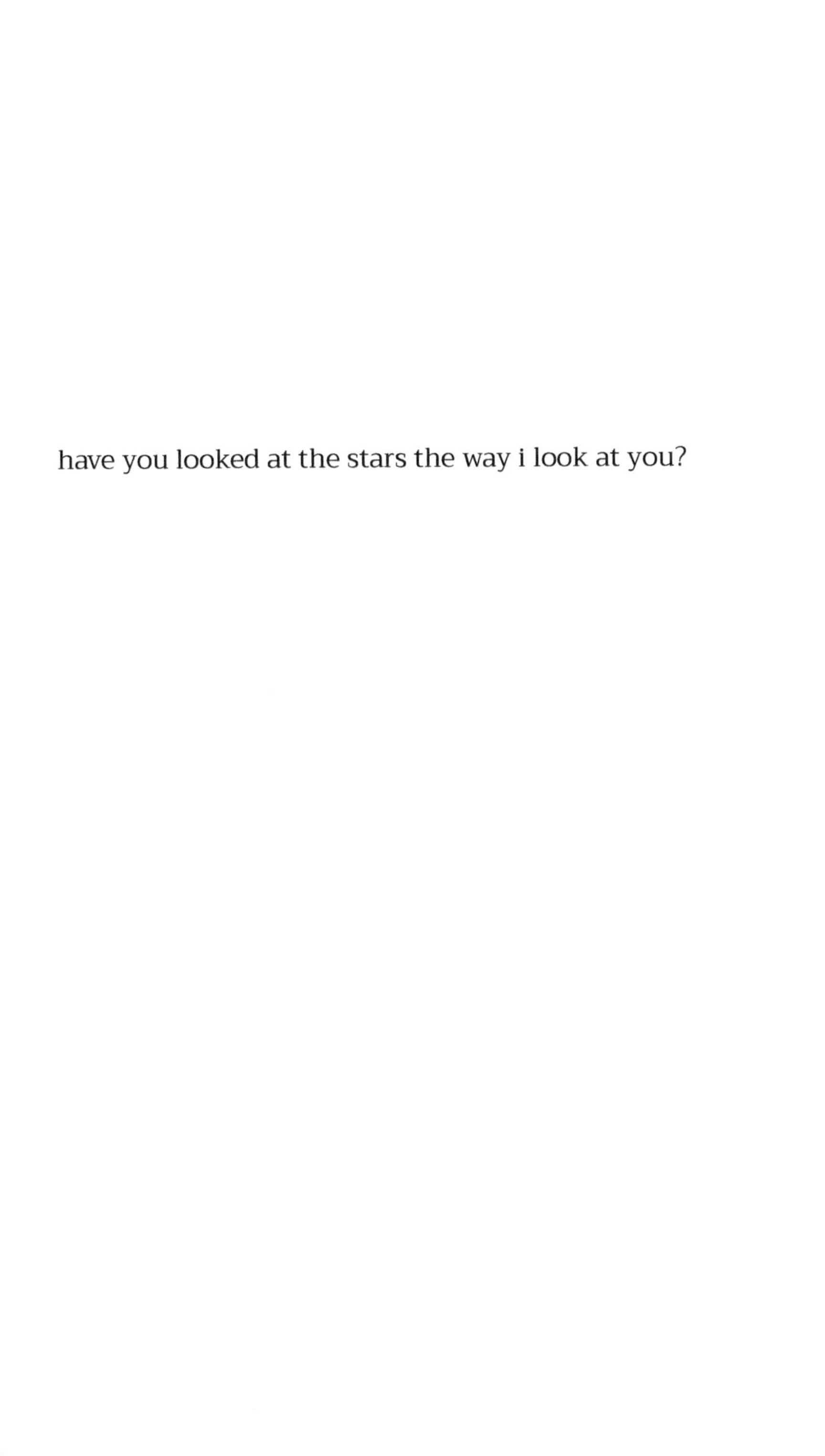
have you looked at the stars the way i look at you?

you are the safe place in which i hide
like a child wishes to hide in the glow
of the moonlight from the dark of night

amber

from the resin of a tree
a healing way to seal up the open wounds
the beauty of the deep colors of the sun and fire
reflecting the hovering trees
the moving restless clouds
the wild birds flying by
yet still translucent
time comes with thunderstorms,
rain, heat, drought
till it weathers the trunk in which it resides
till it snaps off and finds
its way rolling down a clear stream
sinking down to sediment
to find that safe place
to fossilize without interruptions
to close the curtain
when it's time
one will find this treasure
it just took a million years
for it to turn into amber
and to be discovered by the seeker
who knows the value it truly holds
resilient of land and water
preserved with time
found by fate

seasons of life

form me in the sky amongst the clouds

invite

the rain
never lets me stay in
the rain like an old friend
invites you to play
the rain is a gift to be given
by the hand of nature
a blessing on all that it decides to touch
the noise dimming down
from those not willing
to venture out
it feels like an intimate invitation
between you and the droplets
just you and the mist
just you and the sound of nature
clarity from the sky
cleansing for sound of mind

alpha

an alpha will never go down without a fight
never torn from the mission
a mission that its determined pack
will press on with
to destroy evil
to conquer
to fulfill
to live

gather

surrounding me
with evergreen and bunches of bright pink hues
they glisten sparkles of gold when the sunlight
hits just right
whites like the purest of snow
clouds of deep purple that strikes the emotion
of exploring the depths of a dark mysterious forest
i gather myself
upon their presence
drips of scrumptious resin
leave a trace of their fragrance among my fingertips
a peaceful and settling feeling
that arrives by
gathering a petal
a flower bud
a batch of fresh herbs
or bundles of blossoms
and as i sit observing
a joyous contentment trickles in
just by being there with them

*dimming down only to promise a new day to come,
retract only for the waves to return*

modest forest

the forest doesn't need to expose itself like a city does
with bright lights and spaces
with little or no sacredness left to explore
arrows and directions tell you where all avenues are
where they lead to
whereas the forest is only truly revealed
to those who walk in its silence
with an infinite amount to discover
it's off the trail that leads to more
instinct is what navigates you through
not neon signs
it's just you and the wilderness
the stillness and the rain

raining music

it's the rhythm of the rain
when it hits the roof like fingers tapping on a drum
the sound of when it drizzles in melted snow
reminds me of being hidden in the tropical forest
droplets that have just arrived from the clouds
gliding off the emerald,
green leaves onto my skin
every drop amplified,
every drop in sync
when it's raining,
i
listen
to
the
music

gypsy

wind charging
barging in transforming the atmosphere effortlessly
a presence that is meant to be known
without permission
to persist
to play with a lake
toying around
creating waves
people swearing it reminds them of that ocean bay
trees proving their flexibility
mountain dogs on patrol
masked turtles finding shelter
pollen on the loose
spiders locking into their webs
the wind
a passerby
a voyager
a troublemaker
a true gypsy

set the pace of your waves that head for the shore
of your ultimate destination

fern

she was mysterious
as a fern
where only the depths of the forest truly knew her
where she didn't need a spread of erupting colors
she grew
deeply green
serene
for those who step near would be enchanted
by her mystic blade
and her unraveling fiddlehead

whispers

do you ever yearn
to hear the whispers of the forest?
as to tune out the noise that collects in the mind
are we in tune?
truly
without the interference of technology
are we truly here?

under

the best place to be is below the sea
where i am completely submerged and immersed
in the silence
ultimate peace
under the ocean is quiet
but cleverly not
the waves and the sand create a lullaby
the sound of gritty sand rolling back and forth
the sound of dolphins and whales
give a piercing echo in the distance
it's the only amount of noise i want to hear
as the cars and people are muffled by the
protection of waves
if only i could hold my breath forever

fall

the crisp air
the mist of fog
holding the crawling clouds above ground
an orchestra of fallen leaves echo
crunching beneath gripping leather boots
uniformed evergreen trees churn their colors
the palette of a fiery sunset melting into every maple leaf
the valley sprinkled with autumn spice
chimneys raise their signals
homes feel toasty with warm sips and knitted blankets
there is no wonder why i always fall for autumn

spring

strolling down the bleak neighborhood
still in silence from the cold hard winter
i spot a colorful splash
a blossoming flower
my soul springs up
leaping joyfully
a single flower once taken for granted
now savored by nature's delicacy
reviving me
thawing out my heart
one petal at a time

summer

bronzed skin
tinted scenic views
aqua water
celebrating the day
kissing my feet
freckles birthed from the sun
love coming in heat waves
skin revealed
submerged to cool down
citrus lips
from sunup -- till sundown

winter

cool tones
blue hues
cold bones
home body in full mode
heavy layers
of wool and snow
oven overused to bake cookie dough
string lights and frosted porches
starry nights clear the way
for the celebration
of Jesus
a holy winter child
warming up the silent night

owl

while you sleep
i am wide awake
my eyes widen
i stretch my talons
i search for movement
i am on the hunt
the moment the night is mine
i give a hoot to make sure
you know the territory is mine
i'll leave you guessing
where am i
which tree do i reside in
and when you get close,
i'll fly away
into the shine of the moon
leaving you to wonder
what am i
i am but only
a phantom

sacred

a rumbling downpour
of the purest of heavenly water
thunderous soundscape
mighty in presence
continuous in its rhythm
offerings from every drop of rain
chiseling its way into the rocks
engraving its marking through the valley
for those willing to seek its powerful blessing
through the mist
through the clouds
through the ferns
through the trails
there they will be renewed
under the sacred waterfall

sunflower

i hope you bask in the light where it feels like home
i hope your gypsy feet never fail to take you up
to new heights
i hope you live for your dreams
that you've hidden in the shadows
i hope that all your wishes that stem from your heart
grow into more

birdwatching

the steps i take creak upon the wooden porch
overlooking the view of saturated blue
i grip my mug sipping my tea
i hear the forest speak to me
with wild birds native to the land
communicating by song
i want to know their names
i want to identify them by color patterns
they puff out the feathers upon their chest
these birds are messengers of the sky
keeping the growth of the forest
thriving one seed at a time

volcanic

I've turned land into rock
I've burned life in my path
only to create new life
I've slept for many years
while people spoke of my name
some have never seen my fire
my glowing furious lava in full raging force
unable to stop my fury
I'll find my way to the ocean after I erupt
I'll go back to sleep
and all can recover from my explosion
including me
and while you find life of green
from the most fertile of soils
you'll know that was because of me

rascals of the forest

the masked sparrows greet me
at my level
tilting and turning their fluffy heads
chirping their dialect
they peek at me through the shield of twigs
trying to be brave
and I can't help but mimic their language
and for the moment they stay
for the moment they understand me
in an odd way
little rascals of the forest
I am glad I can relate

dragonfly

delicately born in the water
a dragonfly has to survive the gulp of a predator
for a whole year they live in the stream
and after they have survived the odds
they grow their wings,
and they get to take flight into the air
iridescent gold and blues
they reflect the sun and water
glistening a beautiful scene
a dragonfly only lives a month out of the water
a deadline on their flight without knowing
yet they fly and they glide
always staying nearby to
what they always knew
water
a simple and fragile life
water
to air
to dust

firesign

fire upon fire
a fiery rage that can only last for so long
fire upon air
assisting in the spread of the lit wild dragon
fire upon water
always knowing when it's time to simmer down
what is fire
without more fire
what is fire
without air to fuel it
what is fire
without water to put it out